# Sermons for Children
## with Nursery Rhymes and Animals
## of the Bible

## Mark A. Sandell

Parson's Porch Books

*Sermons for Children with Nursery Rhymes and Animals of the Bible*
ISBN: Softcover 978-1-960326-42-3

**Parson's Porch Books** is an imprint of Parson's Porch & Company (PP&C) in Cleveland, Tennessee. PP&C is a self-funded charity which earns money by publishing books of noted authors, representing all genres. Its face and voice is **David Russell Tullock** who you can contact at: dtullock@parsonsporch.com.

Parson's Porch & Company *turns books into bread & milk* by sharing its profits with the poor.

www.parsonsporch.com

# Sermons for Children
with Nursery Rhymes and Animals
of the Bible

# Contents

## Nursery Rhymes

Humpty Dumpty.............................................................7
Humpty Dumpty.............................................................9
Little Bo Peep..............................................................11
Little Bo Peep..............................................................13
Little Bo Peep..............................................................15
Little Bo Peep..............................................................17
For Every Evil.............................................................19
Rain...........................................................................21
Rain...........................................................................23
The Tarts....................................................................25
Miss Muffet................................................................27
Jack and Jill...............................................................29
Pat-A-Cake................................................................31
Pat-A-Cake................................................................33
Little Boy Blue............................................................35
Little Boy Blue............................................................37
Peter Piper.................................................................39
What are Little Boys Made of?....................................41
What are Little Girls Made of? ...................................43
Jack...........................................................................45
Jack...........................................................................47
Baa, Baa, Black Sheep ...............................................49
Birds of a Feather ......................................................51
Birds of a Feather ......................................................53
For Want of a Nail......................................................55
One to Ten ................................................................57
Old Mother Hubbard..................................................59
The Cat and The Fiddle .............................................61

## Animals of the Bible

God Rescues the Animals..............................65
Eagle ................................................................67
Scorpion .........................................................69
Snake or Cobra..............................................71
Whale..............................................................73
Natural Enemies ...........................................75
Bats and Rats ................................................77
Dragon/Leviathan........................................79
Lion..................................................................81
Lion..................................................................83
Camel...............................................................85
Grasshopper ..................................................87
Birds................................................................89
Cranes, Storks, and Doves............................91
Hawk...............................................................93
Leopard/Cheetah..........................................95
Animals of the Bible: Donkey.....................97
Deer .................................................................99
Pig..................................................................101
Pig..................................................................103
Dog ...............................................................105
Fish................................................................107
Fish................................................................109
Unicorn.........................................................111

# Humpty Dumpty

*"Humpty Dumpty sat on a wall, Humpty Dumpty had a great fall; All the King's horses and all the King's men couldn't put Humpty together again."*

**Scripture:** "And the God of all grace, who called you to His eternal glory in Christ, after you have suffered a little while, will himself restore you and make you strong, firm, and steadfast. To Him be the power for ever and ever. Amen." (I Peter 5:10-11).

**Materials Needed:** an egg, a dish to hold it in

We have all had something bad happen to us. Something that's hard and not nice. What are some things that could happen to a person or happened to you that was bad? (Children give their responses)

In one of our nursery rhymes, something bad happened. Listen to the nursery rhyme to hear what happened. This large egg named Humpty Dumpty was sitting on a wall and then he fell. What happens when an egg falls or is dropped? Let me show it to you. (Drop egg in the dish) That is right, it breaks. Can you put the egg back together again? You can try but it is quite a mess. That sure is something bad that happened.

Then what happened in the story? All the King's men and all the King's horses came to put Humpty back together. Do you think they would be able to do this? No. No matter how hard they tried; they could not put this large egg back together.

Who would you call to help when something bad happened? (answers). The one who can help the most is the King who created you. The problem with Humpty Dumpty is that he called the King's horses and the King's men. He should have called the King to come and help him. The King, God, Jesus, could truly put Humpty together again because He created Humpty.

This is what Peter meant when he shared this scripture with us. Let me share the scripture with you. (Read scripture). When we are in trouble, we need to talk to our parents, pastor, Sunday School teacher, friends, but let us not forget that we need the King to help us as well. God can help us with whatever problem we may face. Whatever bad thing that has happened to us, God can help us get through it.

Prayer: *Dear God, thank you for listening to us and for helping us with our problems. We know that no matter what happens, you can get us through it. In Christ's name, we pray, Amen.*

# Humpty Dumpty

*"Humpty Dumpty sat on a wall; Humpty Dumpty
had a great fall; Humpty Dumpty shouted, "Amen!
God can put me together again."*

**Scripture:** "If anyone is in Christ, they are a new
creation." (II Corinthians 5:17)

**Materials Needed:** an egg.

We have all had something bad happen to us.
Something that's hard and not nice. What are
some things that could happen to a person or
happened to you that was bad? *(Children responses)*

In one of our nursery rhymes, something bad
happened. Listen to the nursery rhyme to hear what
happened. This large egg named Humpty Dumpty was
sitting on a wall and then he fell. What happens when
an egg falls or is dropped? That is right, it breaks. Can
you put the egg back together again? You can try but
it is quite a mess. That sure is something bad that
happened.

With God, even when something bad happens, God
can make it all right again. We can't put this egg back
together again. But God can. God can do amazing
things. What are some of the miracles that you
remember from the Bible? *(Children responses)*

Those are great responses. We have heard out of the Bible how God can make all things new. We have heard how God can do amazing things. God can even make us new again. I would like to share with you a new kind of nursery rhyme about Humpty Dumpty, focusing on how God can make us new. (*Share the nursery rhyme.*) In this rhyme, God performed a miracle. He put Humpty Dumpty, an egg, back together again. That is a miracle from an amazing God.

God can do that with us. God can take us with all our heart ache and pain and put us back together again. He can forgive our sins and make us new again. The Apostle Paul wrote about this to the church in Corinth in his second letter. Here is what he wrote. (*Read the Scripture.*)

Did you hear that? When we accept Jesus Christ as our Savior, we are made brand new. Now does God take away all our wrinkles? No, not really. We are made brand new in our heart and how we live. We now can love God and love others, all because God has given us a second chance.

**Prayer:** *We thank You, great God, for Your great love and how You make us brand new again and again. Help us to accept Jesus into our hearts so that we can live for You. In the name of our Savior, Jesus Christ, Amen.*

# Little Bo Peep

*"Little Bo Peep has lost her sheep and can't tell where to find them; Leave them alone, and they'll come home, and bring their tails behind them."*

**Scripture:** "Then Jesus told them this parable: Suppose one of you has a hundred sheep and loses one of them. Does he not leave the ninety-nine in the open country and go after the lost sheep until he finds it? And when he finds it, he joyfully puts it on his shoulders and goes home. Then he calls his friends and neighbors together and says, `Rejoice with me; I have found my lost sheep.' I tell you that in the same way there will be more rejoicing in heaven over one sinner who repents than over ninety-nine righteous persons who do not need to repent." (Luke 15:3-7)

**Materials Needed:** a stuffed sheep and maybe a shepherd's staff.

Have you ever lost anything? (*Children's responses.*) Have you ever been lost? What did it feel like? (Responses—made me sad, cried, etc.) Have you ever heard of a girl named Little Bo Peep? She was a girl in a nursery rhyme that lost her sheep. She couldn't find them. Her nursery rhyme goes like this, "Little Bo Peep has lost her sheep, and can't tell where to find them; Leave them alone, and they'll come home, and bring their tails behind them."

The advice given to Little Bo Peep is for her to wait, and the sheep will come home on their own. The problem with this advice is that sheep don't have a GPS. In fact, sheep don't always come home because sheep can get lost easily. Little Bo Peep is not being a shepherd. A shepherd goes and finds the lost sheep and then brings them home.

Let me share with you a story about a real shepherd— Jesus. (Share scripture).

Jesus shared with us that when we are lost, he searches for us. When we are lost in our sin, He comes to find us and then brings us home. Jesus as the great shepherd seeks us out because He knows that we can get lost, that we can be frightened, that our GPS as a human sometimes is broken. He looks for us. And when we are found, there is great rejoicing.

This is why the church exists—we are to look for those who are lost. That is what Jesus has asked us to do— go and find the lost sheep, the lost people and bring them home—into the church and into the kingdom of heaven.

**Prayer:** *Dear God, we thank you for giving us Jesus the great shepherd who looks for us when we are lost and then takes us home when we are found. In the precious name of Jesus we pray, Amen.*

# Little Bo Peep

*"Little Bo Peep has lost her sheep and can't tell where to find them; Leave them alone, and they'll come home, and bring their tails behind them."*

**Scripture:** "The LORD is my shepherd, I shall not be in want. He makes me lie down in green pastures, he leads me beside quiet waters, he restores my soul. He guides me in paths of righteousness for his name's sake." (Psalm 23:1-3)

**Materials Needed:** A stuffed sheep.

Do you remember Little Bo Peep? Can anyone share the nursery rhyme about her with the rest of us? (sharing) Today I want to talk about another shepherd. King David. King David wrote a song. We know it as a psalm. It was about a Great Shepherd, a Great Shepherd that we know as God. The first two lines of his song goes like this, "The Lord is my shepherd, I shall not want. He makes me to lie down in green pastures, He leads me beside quiet waters, He restores my soul."

In this psalm we are asked to make the Lord our shepherd. God is to be the One who leads us and guides us. And God will take better care of us than Little Bo Peep in the nursery rhyme.

In the story of Little Bo Peep, the sheep are lost and Little Bo Peep, their shepherd, doesn't know where they are. In the song that King David wrote, that is not the case. The Lord as our Shepherd knows where we his sheep are. In fact, the Lord knows us so well that He asks us to take some time to rest. That is what was meant in the psalm when we heard, "He makes us to lie down in green pastures and besides still waters. " An amazing thing about rest is that once we take time to relax, we are calmed and refreshed.

What do some of you do to relax? (Answers, also add some of your own). Did you notice in the song that sometimes God as the shepherd makes us relax? God is so concerned about us that He not only knows where we are, but He makes us take time to relax. He makes us slow down.

**Prayer:** *Dear God, we thank you that we ask us to relax, to take some time to slow down and to calm down. We are blessed when we slow down because You refresh us. We thank you that we have a Great Shepherd in Jesus, in whose name we pray, Amen.*

# Little Bo Peep

*"Little Bo Peep has lost her sheep and can't tell where to find them; Leave them alone, and they'll come home, and bring their tails behind them."*

**Scripture:** "The Lord is my Shepherd...Even though I walk through the valley of the shadow of death, I will fear no evil, for you are with me; your rod and your staff, they comfort me." (Psalm 23:4)

**Materials Needed:** a stuffed sheep and a shepherd's staff.

I would like to share a nursery rhyme with you. It is about Little Bo Peep. Does anyone remember who she is? She is the shepherd that has lost her sheep. Let us listen to the rhyme and she what she did. (Share the rhyme). Did you hear her advice about what to do with lost sheep? She will wait until the sheep come home on their own.

We know of another shepherd that is way more concerned about us than Little Bo Peep. This shepherd is the Lord. King David said that when we make the Lord our shepherd that He not only seeks after us if we are lost but he also comes to protect us if we face terrible things.

What are some terrible things that a sheep may face? (Answers such as wolf, lion, etc.) A shepherd is supposed to come to the rescue of those sheep that are lost, saving them from danger. How does a shepherd do this? With the rod and staff. Using his staff, a shepherd would rescue the sheep that were in need like this (use the crook to pick up the stuffed sheep). Or the shepherd would fight off enemies with the staff (pretend to fight off a lion).

God said that He is our shepherd and comes to help us when something bad happens. He will guard us from enemies with the power of his staff and simply by being with us.

Listen to how King David sang about his shepherd. (Share the scripture)

What are some of the bad things that could happen to us? (Answers—a bully, family member dies, etc.) And do you know that God helps us when these things happen. He helps us through the church and the loving care of church members and other caring adults.

And if someone dies, Jesus Christ is there to take them to God. Jesus will make certain that those who believe will go home to heaven to be with God.

**Prayer:** *Dear God, we are not afraid when bad things happen because we know that You are with us. We thank you for Jesus, our loving Shepherd, Amen.*

# Little Bo Peep

*"Little Bo Peep has lost her sheep and can't tell where to find them; Leave them alone, and they'll come home, and bring their tails behind them."*

**Scripture:**" I am the good shepherd; I know my sheep and my sheep know me." (John 10:14)

**Materials Needed:** stuffed sheep.

Do all of you have names? Of course, you do! We have names that have been given to us by our parents that we use each day. We also have names that have been given to us because of who we are or what we have done. I am called Pastor (or Mr. or Mrs. or Ms. as appropriate). As a result of my degree and being called here to serve, you know me as Pastor. Some people also give us nicknames. Do any of you have a nickname? (*Children's responses.*)

There is a nursery rhyme that has a shepherd losing her sheep. She can't find them, nor does she seem to know their names. The rhyme goes like this— (share the Little Bo Peep nursery rhyme). How would she find them if she doesn't know their name? She would try— Come little sheep?! That doesn't seem to work very well. If you were to lose your pet, you would go and look for it and call your pet by name.

Well, I am glad to tell you that Someone from heaven knows your name—even if you are lost. Jesus said that He was the Good Shepherd. He is such a great shepherd that He knows His sheep. He knows us so well that He can call us by name. He knows us so well that He even knows the number of hairs on our head. He knows even the smallest of details about who we are.

He knows us, and even if we are lost, He will come to search for us. When we feel alone, He will come and be with us. If we are hurting, He will listen to us. If we are in pain, Jesus will come to help us and heal us.

Little Bo Peep can't be there for us, but Jesus can. Jesus our Savior will help us when we are in need because He is also our Great Shepherd.

**Prayer:** *Dear Caring God, we thank you for wanting to know everything about us. You know when we are safe and when we are lost. And when we are lost, you come looking for us, calling us by name, seeking for us, until we are brought back to you. We praise you for our Shepherd, Jesus, in whose name we pray, Amen.*

# For Every Evil

*"For every evil under the sun, there is a remedy or there is none. If there be one, seek till you find it; if there be none, never mind it."*

**Scripture:** "Do not repay anyone evil for evil...Do not be overcome by evil but overcome evil with good." (Romans 12:17, 21).

**Materials Needed:** none.

We have been talking about nursery rhymes and how they teach us about the Bible and about Jesus. I have a little known one that I would like to share with you. (Share "For Every Evil").

This nursery rhyme talks about looking, looking for the answer to the problem that we know as evil in the world. It says that maybe we will not find an answer on how to deal with evil. Can anyone tell me what evil is? (Responses such as when someone hurts another on purpose, people who hate and hurt, etc.)

I would like to tell you about a person I know who had to deal with lots of evil. His name is Paul, the apostle Paul. There were many people who did not want to hear about what he said about Jesus. These people didn't like what Paul had to say so much that they beat him, threw stones at him, threw him out of cities, hit him with sticks, threw him in prison and tried to have him killed. What do you think that Paul would say on how to deal with these mean people? (responses)

19

Let me share with you what he wrote on how to deal with evil. He did not say that we should give up if we cannot find a solution—like the nursery rhyme says. Paul wrote this to the church in Rome, (share scripture).

Instead of hurting someone because they hurt you, we are asked to be like God and Jesus. We are to show love. Love is the greatest tool that God has given to us to use when we deal with people who have hurt. The first step of love is to forgive them. Next, we are to ask God to forgive them. Then we are to do positive actions that can change them (you can at this point ask the young people for actions that they can do to show love)—compliment them, don't talk bad about them, treat them with kindness. This is how Jesus loved the whole world when it didn't love him—he showed his great love through His forgiveness and kindness.

**Prayer:** *Dear forgiving God, we are grateful that You give us the strength to love others like You have loved us. May we do so for Jesus and so that we can show Jesus to others, in His wonderful name, Amen.*

# Rain

*"Rain, Rain, go away, come again another day. Little Johnny wants to play".*

**Scripture:** Genesis 6-8

**Materials Needed:** a shoe box.

Let me share a nursery rhyme with you. It is about rain. Anyone know this one? Well, here it is (share the rhyme). How do you feel when it rains?

There was a group of people in the Bible who probably felt like Little Johnny. Any guesses who that may have been? They were on a great big boat. It rained for forty days and nights. That's right—we are talking about Noah and his family. On this ark, Noah, his wife, his three sons, their wives, eight total people, and…what else was on the ark? That is right—animals—all kinds of animals. There was at least one pair of every animal on the face of the earth.

Why do think that it rained for so long? (answers) The problem was that the humans got bad—mean, cruel, and hateful. The people had gotten far away from what God wanted them to be as loving, caring, and pure. So, God decided that he would pick a kind and nice family and start all over again.

Since animals were a gift from God, God was not going to destroy them as well. So, God instructed Noah to build a great big boat in order to save his family and all of the animals. The boat or ark according to the dimensions in the Bible would have been a big rectangular box, like a shoe box (show the shoe box). The reason for this is that when the waves would hit the boat, they couldn't knock it over.

Now in Noah's time it rained a lot. Anyone remember how many days? How many nights? (40). That is a lot of rain. So much rain fell that the whole earth was covered with water. The reason that water was used is the same reason that you use water when you take a bath—it cleans. Water cleans you in the tub or shower, and it cleaned the whole earth during the time of Noah.

After that God said that the whole world would never be destroyed with water. As a sign of God's promise, God put a rainbow in the sky. So, every time we see a rainbow, we can know that God keeps His promise.

**Prayer:** *Dear God, we thank You for rain and what it means to us. We thank You for your promises found in rainbows. We also thank you for the promise found in Jesus that You save us from our sins. In the name of the Savior, we pray, Amen.*

# Rain

*"Rain, Rain, go away, come again another day. Little Johnny wants to play".*

**Scripture:** Genesis 6-8

**Materials Needed:** a glass of water, a picture of a well

How many of you like rain? What can you do in the rain? The one sharing this nursery rhyme thinks that you cannot do much when it is raining. The nursery rhyme about little Johnny is that he cannot play when it is raining. (Share the nursery rhyme).

Why do you think that we need rain? (Responses— waters plants, grass, trees; need for drinking etc.) God in His greatness made the world in such a way that it continues to renew itself. The sun warms the earth so that things can grow. It gives light so that we can see. The rain waters the earth so that we have drinking water and plants can grow. Snow also waters the earth so that we have water.

Water is one of the basic items that we need to live. We humans are made up mostly of water, so we need to drink lots of it.

Jesus had something to say about water. He was at a well in an area called Samaria. A well is a deep hole with water at the bottom of it. It was the middle of the day, and few people were there. In fact, there was only one woman. Jesus asked her for a drink of water. She was surprised that Jesus, a Jew, was talking to her a Samaritan woman. Jesus then told her that He was the one who had Living Water. She could not understand the difference between His water and the water in the well.

All water does give life—so what was Jesus talking about? Living Water? (children's responses). That is right. When we accept Jesus as Savior and take Him into our hearts, He waters our soul. He helps us to deal with the problems of life. Jesus gives us the strength to deal with the bully at our school, or to pick our spirits up when we are down, or to help us be kind to each other. Living water means that we can live life with Jesus watering our soul so that we can grow in faith.

**Prayer:** *Dear God, we are grateful that you provide rain which helps plants grow and that you give the sun to warm us and the world. We also thank You for the Living Water that we find in Jesus who gives us life and strength. It is in the name of Jesus we pray, Amen.*

# The Tarts

*"The Queen of Hearts, She made some tarts, All on a summer's day; The Knave of Hearts, He stole the tarts, and took them away(verse one)*

*The King of Hearts called for the tarts, and beat the Knave full sore; The Knave of Hearts brought back the tarts and vowed he would steal no more (verse two)."*

**Scripture:** The Ten Commandments, Exodus 20:1-17

**Materials Needed:** a picture of a tart, a small pie, or an apple turnover

What if you had something and someone took it away—what would that be? (children's response—stealing) Yes, that would be stealing. So, what is wrong with that? (children's responses—it is mine, stealing is wrong, etc.) One of ten commandments says that "Thou shall not steal." Stealing is certainly wrong—here on earth and in heaven.

Let us listen a nursery rhyme and see what it says about stealing. (Share the first verse of the rhyme which is above). What is a tart? Oh, that is a delicious little kind of pie. It is sweet and tasty. The Knave stole the pie and thought he got away with it. Even if someone does steal and is not caught, does he get away with it? No, God will make certain that all is made right—whether in this life or next.

Let me share the rest of the rhyme with you and listen to what happens to the Knave (share verse two). The King caught him and made certain that the Knave knew he had done wrong. And the Knave brought back the tarts and learned the lesson—do not steal.

In our lives as Christians, we are asked to follow the right ways of God. We are asked to follow the Ten Commandments so that we can have a good relationship with God and with other humans. One of the great reasons that we attend church and Sunday School is to help each other so that we do not act like the Knave in the nursery rhyme. Here at our church, we remind each other about what is good and right and how we are to live. Your Sunday School teachers share the good news and help you to make Godly decisions. In worship, we share about Jesus and how He wants us to follow with our hearts and in our lives.

**Prayer:** *Dear God, we ask that you help us help each other to become like You. As we work together, may we follow You with our words and our actions, in Jesus, we pray, Amen.*

# Miss Muffet

*"Little Miss Muffet sat on a tuffet, eating her curds and whey; Along came a spider and sat down beside her, And frightened Miss Muffet away."*

**Scripture:** "I come to face you in the name of the Lord God Almighty. (I Samuel 17:45)

"Look at the birds of the air; they do not sow or reap or store away in barns, and yet your heavenly Father feeds them. Are you not much more valuable than they? Who of you by worrying can add a single hour to his life?" (Matthew 6:26-27).

**Materials Needed:** a cottage cheese container, full or empty; a stool

How many of you have ever been afraid? What are some things that scare you or may scare others? (answers). Well, I would like to tell you a story about someone who was afraid. Her name was Miss Muffet—a little girl who was just sitting minding her own business when she was scared, scared so much that she ran away.

Listen to this rhyme titled "Miss Muffet". (Share the nursery rhyme. After sharing the nursery rhyme, make certain to share what curds and whey are which are cottage cheese and what is a tuffet is which is a low stool.)

Would you be afraid if a spider sat down beside you? I sure would. I would like now to share a story with you about a little boy who should have been afraid but was not. His name was David, and he was asked to face a giant, not a little spider. Does anyone remember the name of the giant—that's right, it was Goliath. The Bible says that Goliath was nine feet tall. Now I am (insert height) and Goliath would have been almost twice as tall as me. David was going to face him in a battle. Goliath had a shield, a sword and wore a helmet. David only had a sling and five stones. It doesn't sound like it will be much of a fight.

Yet David was not afraid. In fact, David did not run away like Miss Muffet. Does anyone know why David was not afraid? Let me share it with you out of the Bible (read I Samuel 17:45). David was not afraid because he was on God's side.

In the New Testament, Jesus shared with us the reason why we can trust God, why we don't need to be afraid. In His sermon on the mountain, Jesus shared this with us, (read Matthew 6:26-27)

David showed us that we need to trust that God will protect us. Jesus said that God loves us so much that God will watch over us and care for us.

**Prayer:** *Dear God, Thank you for watching over us and for protecting us. Help us to follow You and in following You, help us not to be afraid. In Jesus' name, Amen.*

# Jack and Jill

*"Jack and Jill went up the hill to fetch a pail of water;*
*Jack fell down and broke his crown, and*
*Jill came tumbling after."*

**Scripture:** "A friend loves at all times. "(Proverbs 17:17)

**Materials Needed:** a picture of two friends.

Have you ever had such a good friend that you did everything together? What are some of the things that you shared? (Listen and comment on the different things that the youth share).

There is a nursery rhyme about good friends. It is called Jack and Jill. Does anyone know it? (If someone knows it, have them share it; otherwise share the nursery rhyme with the children.) Poor Jack. He fell down the hill and broke his crown. The crown would be his head. He hurt his head.

And did you hear what Jill did. She shared in his pain. She went down the hill after him, to help him, to make certain that he was okay, and if he was not okay, to get some medical help.

There is a proverb that fits this. It is one of those easy memory verses. It is Proverbs 17:17 and it goes like this, "A friend loves at all times." A friend loves you when things are going well, and a good friend loves you even when things are not going well like if you fell down and hurt yourself.

Now what do you think Jill did to help Jack? I ask this so that we can know how to help someone we love who is hurting. (Responses of the children). That is right—we can get medical help and/or we can tell parents that something bad happened. We can cry with them—it is important that we share all things with friends—even to cry together. We can try and comfort them with kind words. We can let them lean on us if they are unable to walk. All these actions show that we care and that we are a good friend.

**Prayer:** *Dear God, we thank you for friends, especially those who help us when we are hurt or sad and who stand by us no matter what may happen. Help us also to be a friend like Jill who was there for Jack. And we thank you for Jesus, our greatest friend. We pray in His name, Amen.*

# Pat-A-Cake

*"Pat-a-cake, pat-a-cake, Baker's Man!*
*Bake me a cake as fast as you can.*
*Pat it, and prick it and*
*Mark it with a T, and*
*Put it in the oven for Tommy and me."*

**Scripture:** I Thessalonians 5:18

**Materials Needed:** none.

Listen to this nursery rhyme— (share the rhyme as listed above). Have you ever heard this one before? Have you ever done this one? (On the pat a part, your hands are put together like praying; on the cake part, you cross over to the person in front of you and make praying hands; this is repeated using the other hand with the first two lines. The next part is "pat it" which would be a pat on the head. The "prick it" would be a finger point to the tummy area and this is also the area that the T is drawn. The rhyme ends with sharing the last line. After the motions are shared, you would share the symbolism of the rhyme.)

Notice that when we are patting the cake, we are making praying hands. This shows us that all we try to do, we are to ask God's blessing upon it. We pray over all that we do from getting ready for a test to going to bed to before we share in a meal to getting ready for a sports event. All that we try, we should ask God's blessing on it.

Did you see that we did it again and again? Praying once is not enough. We need to ask God again and again for His blessings. Is this because God didn't hear the first time? No, this is so we are reminded that it was God who blessed us. We humans often forget God, so we need to pray again and again to God so that we know that it is God who helps us.

The next part is to pat and prick and mark with a T. We also need to remember that we are to show our love for each other through touch. Jesus showed this time and again as when he healed people, he touched them with His hands. We need to follow Jesus in His example and touch those who are hurting with hugs and pat those on the back who have done great things.

As we pray and love, we do this in the name of the one who truly touched us, Jesus Christ.

**Prayer:** *Dear God, we are grateful for our many blessings. Help us to remember to care for others as You have cared for us in Jesus, Amen.*

# Pat-A-Cake

*"Pat-a-cake, pat-a-cake, Baker's Man!*
*Bake me a cake as fast as you can.*
*Pat it, and prick it and*
*Mark it with a T, and*
*Put it in the oven for Tommy and me."*

**Scripture:** "The King will reply, `I tell you the truth, whatever you did for one of the least of these brothers of mine, you did for me.'" (Matthew 25:40)

**Materials Needed:** a cake mix box.

Listen to this nursery rhyme— (share the rhyme as listed above). Have you ever heard this one before? Have you ever done this one? (This one has motions—on the pat a part, your hands are put together like praying; on the cake part, you cross over to the person in front of you and make praying hands; this is repeated using the other hand with the first two lines. The next part is "pat it" which would be a pat on the head. The "prick it" would be a finger point to the tummy area and this is also the area that the T is drawn. The rhyme ends with sharing the last line. After the motions are shared, you would share the symbolism of the rhyme.)

The motions make this a fun rhyme to share. But there are other parts that are fun as well. How many of you love the smell of a cake baking? Me too. I don't know of too many others great smells than that of a cake baking in the oven (smell deeply as if smelling the thought of a cake baking).

This nursery rhyme is about sharing. Did you hear that we are not baking a cake just for ourselves—we are baking a cake for...? Tommy as well.

The church is a lot like the baker. We don't just share with ourselves. We are looking beyond our walls to see how we can touch the world with what God has given to us. What are some of the ways in which we can share with those in need in our world?
(Answers such as helping the poor, concern for creation, food for those who need it, etc.)

When we as the church help those around us, we become like Jesus who helped those around Him. We are to help as Jesus helped.

**Prayer:** *Dear God, we thank you for cakes and goodies and the ability to make them and eat them. Help us to share our cakes and other things with those in need. We ask this in the name of our Savior, Jesus, Amen.*

# Little Boy Blue

*"Little Boy Blue, come, blow your horn!*
*The sheep's in the meadow, the cow's in the corn.*
*Where's the little boy that looks after the sheep?*
*Under the haystack, fast asleep!"*

**Scripture:** "Whatever you do, work at it with all your heart, as working for the Lord." (Colossians 3:23)

**Materials Needed:** a musical instrument

How many of you like music? What kind of music do you like? What is your favorite song? Thank you for all your responses.

I have got a story of a little boy whose name was Little Boy Blue who was good at playing the trumpet. There was only one problem with that—he sometimes forgot to play. Can you imagine what worship would be like if our organist forgot what song she was playing and halfway through the song, she started playing another song or she simply forgot to play at all. That would be weird. Or if halfway through our next hymn, this side of the congregation decided to sing something else— that would be chaos.

Well, one time this little boy in the nursery rhyme forgot to play, and it was chaos. Let me share the story with you— (share the nursery rhyme). Did you hear what happened? The sheep are still wandering in the meadow and the cows are rumbling through the corn and creating chaos. All because someone forgot to do their job.

The Apostle Paul had something to say about responsibility—he wrote to the church in Colossae that whatever we do, we are to do it with the focus of doing the best job possible. Paul wrote it this way, "Whatever you do, work at it with all your heart, as working for the Lord." (Colossians 3:23) The best way to live, the best way to do a job is to do it for a greater purpose— as you serve the Lord Jesus Christ. When we have this focus of serving the Lord, then we will not forget, and we will be able to do our best.

**Prayer:** *Dear God, we want to do our best for you. Help us to do our best no matter what we do especially when we work for others. We do thank you for the one who did His best for us always, Jesus, and it is in His name that we pray, Amen.*

# Little Boy Blue

*"Little Boy Blue, come, blow your horn!*
*The sheep is in the meadow, the cow's in the corn.*
*Where's the little boy that looks after the sheep?*
*Under the haystack, fast asleep!"*

**Scripture:** Matthew 25:14-30

**Materials Needed:** a musical instrument

Have you ever met someone who had musical talent? We are blessed to have talented musical people in our church (name some of the people or areas in which there is musical talent in the church and then share who blessed the church is to have these people ministering in the church).

Well, I want you to meet a boy who had talent. His talent was so great that when he played, not only did people marvel but the animals gathered around. Can you imagine being so good that when you played an instrument, even the animals appreciated it and came running to hear it.

Let me share the story about this little boy. (Share the nursery rhyme). Did you hear it? The animals gathered around—you heard that, right? You didn't?! What really happened? (Responses of the children).

Oh!! That is right! Little Boy Blue was asleep in the haystack! That is right—he didn't use his talent. The

37

sad end result is that the animals were not able to gather to hear the great music.

There is a Bible story about that. Jesus told the story of us using our talents. He said that there were three men—each given a different number of talents—in the Bible story, this meant money. Each man used the talents in a different way. The one given five talents increased them to ten. The one given three talents increased the talents to six and the one given one talent, well, he still had one talent at the end of the story. Jesus praised two of the three men. Any guesses as to which ones He praised? The men who used their talents. The man who did nothing with his talent was not praised.

Little Boy Blue in the nursery rhyme also didn't use his talents and well, there was a sad ending to the story. Jesus asks us to use the talents given to us so that we can bless others and so that God gets the glory.

**Prayer:** *Dear God, we appreciate the talents that you have given to each of us. Help us to use our talents to know more about You and to tell others about You. In Jesus name, Amen.*

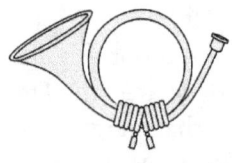

# Peter Piper

*"Peter Piper picked a peck of pickled peppers.*
*A peck of pickled peppers Peter Piper picked.*
*If Peter Piper picked a peck of pickled peppers,*
*Where's the peck of pickled peppers Peter Piper picked?"*

**Scripture:** "If we confess our sins, he is faithful and just and will forgive us our sins and purify us from all unrighteousness." (I John 1:9)

**Materials Needed:** a jar of peppers, a copy of the rhyme for the children

Does anyone know what a tongue twister is? A tongue twister is a saying that is meant to work your tongue so hard in saying words that some words get all mixed up. It is hard work saying a tongue twister—especially if you try and say it fast. (you may also do as a repeat response)

I have a tongue twister in my hand. Do I have a volunteer who would want to try and say this saying and say it fast? (Depending on time, one to three may try). That was hard to try and say it fast.

Just to share a few thoughts about the nursery rhyme. Peter Piper is the boy's name. He is picking peppers so that the peppers may be canned or stored for future use. And it is amazing when you put so many the same kind of sounding words in a sentence, how hard that makes it to say.

There are some people who can share this rhyme and do it fast (either try and share it fast or say that this was a talent God didn't bless you with. If you are able to share it, then say). Now was I able to do this just by looking at it? No, I took hours to practice this tongue twister. I did fail many times, but I continued to try.

This reminds me of something that the Bible tells us—if we fail at something, we get second chances. Or if we commit a sin, then we can come to God, asking for forgiveness and God does forgive us—we get a chance to try again. This is found in many places in the Bible but for today, I would like to share a verse out of I John.

(Share the scripture)

God gives us second and third and fourth and more chances to get out lives right with Him, just like when we try tongue twisters. All we must do when we fail or commit a sin, is to ask for forgiveness and try and try again.

**Prayer:** *Dear God, we do praise you for the many chances that we get from You. Help us to do better each time that we try so that we can be more like Jesus, in whose name we pray, Amen.*

# What are Little Boys Made of?

*What are little boys made of? Slugs and snails and puppy-dogs' tail, that's what little boys are made of.*

**Scripture:** "So God created humans in His own image, in the image of God the human were created; male and female God created them." (Genesis 1:27)

**Materials Needed:** a picture of a snail.

Today we are going to look at how God created humans. We are first going to look at the way in which boys were created. Does anyone remember the name of the first boy in the Bible? That's right, it was Adam. His name, Adam, means man so God created the first boy and named him man or Adam.

Now the tough question is what boys are made of. I have a nursery rhyme that describes boys, and it goes like this. (Share the rhyme). You heard what the rhyme says what boys are made of, do you agree? Are boys made of snips and snails and puppy dog tails?

(Responses of the children).

No, of course they are not made from snips, which are little pieces of things like a broken pencil or an arrowhead. Nor are they made from snails because boys tend to run and run fast. And I don't think that they are made from puppy dog tails. That thought is cruel and crazy.

So, what are boys made of? How did God make a human? Let me share this Bible verse with you that comes from Genesis. Genesis is the first book of our Bible and means beginnings. So, in this first book, God told us how He created the human. Let me share this scripture with you. (Read Genesis 1:26) Instead of making humans like all the other animals or even making humans like each other, we are made in God's image. An image is like what you see in the mirror. An image is like a reflection.

So, what do you think it means that we are made in the image of God? (Responses need to be that we reflect who God is or that we show the goodness and greatness of God). Our responsibility is to show who God is to the world—not be snaps or snails or even puppy dog tails.

**Prayer:** *Dear God, thank you that we are made in your image and that we are to show your goodness to those around us. In the name of Jesus Christ, we pray, Amen.*

# What are Little Girls Made of?

*"What are little girls made of, made of? What are little girls made of? Sugar and spice and everything nice, and That's what little girls are made of."*

**Scripture:** "Then God said, 'Let us make the human in our image and in our likeness, ...so God created humans; male and female God created them." (Genesis 1:26).

**Materials Needed:** a bag of sugar or something sweet.

There is an interesting nursery rhyme about how humans are made. (If you do this as a two-part series, reference the boy part as well). The rhyme asks the question what little girls are made of. What do you think, what are little girls made of? (Responses). Well, the rhyme doesn't agree with you. It goes like this. (Read the rhyme).

What do you think, are girls made of sugar and spice and everything nice? (Have some fun with what the children say). According to the Bible, it agrees with you. Girls are not made with sugar or spice or even everything nice. Instead, girls along with boys are made very different than that. In fact, according to the book of Genesis, we are made very different from the other creatures on the earth. When it said how the creatures were created, it was after their own kind. What this means is that all categories of creatures look like each other. Cows will always be cows. Chickens will always look like chickens.

However, it is different with us humans, girls and boys. We are made in the image of God. (Share the scripture). We humans are made in the image and likeness of God. What this means is that we are supposed to show what God looks like to the world. When people see us, it would be like a mirror that people investigate and see God. What are some ways in which we can show God to others? (Responses such as be kind, help others, be caring, help around the house, come to church, are all appropriate).

**Prayer:** *Dear God, what a great gift that we are to show You to the world. May you help us to be kind and generous as live out the love of Your Son. It is in the blessed name of Jesus that we pray, Amen.*

# Jack

*"Jack be nimble, Jack be quick,
Jack jump over the candlestick."*

**Scripture:** "You are the light of the world. A city on a hill cannot be hidden. Neither do people light a lamp and put it under a bowl. Instead, they put it on its stand, and it gives light to everyone in the house." (Matthew 5:14-15)

**Materials Needed:** a candle and a bowl or basket to hide it in.

How many of you like when it is dark? What happens when it is dark? (Response—you can't see, scary, etc.). That is right, one of the things that happen when there is no light is that you can't see. We need light in order to live life.

Today's nursery rhyme is about light. Actually, it is about a boy named Jack who wanted to jump over a candlestick. (Read the rhyme). Now why do you think that Jack wanted to jump over a candlestick, a lit candlestick? (answers) I don't know either. What would happen if Jack was slow jumping over the candlestick? He would have gotten burned. But he also could have put the candle out like this (quickly put the bowl over the candle so that it goes out).

Now if Jack put the light out, we can't see. There is a scripture that talks about this. (Read the scripture). Jesus was trying to tell us not to put our lights out.

People need to see that God is real in our lives and that God's love rules in our lives.

What are some of the ways that we can show our light? What are some of the ways that we can show that God is real in our lives? (Answers focused on doing good things because Christ has made us good.)

**Prayer:** *We thank you Almighty God for asking us to be light. Help us to shine for you as we seek to help others, be kind to our brothers and sisters, listen to our parents, and help other children who are afraid and alone. Help us to be the light of this world, showing how you have touched us. We ask this prayer in the name of the light of God, Jesus Christ, Amen.*

# Jack

*"Jack be nimble, Jack be quick,*
*Jack jump over the candlestick."*

**Scripture:** "I have told you these things, so that in me you may have peace. In this world you will have trouble. But take heart! I have overcome the world." (John 16:33)

**Materials Needed:** Two construction paper hearts.

There are some sad things in this world, things that make you cry. What are some things that can make you cry? (As each youth shares, tear off a part of one of the hearts) When sad things happen, it can feel like our heart is hurting, like our heart is breaking.

There is a nursery rhyme about this. (Read the rhyme). The problem Jack had was to get from one side of the room to the other. The candle was in the way, so Jack just jumped over the candle and the candlestick.

Jesus had something to say about this as well and the sadness we can feel. He said that there are sad things in this world but that we are to remember that He is stronger than those things that make us sad. Here is what He said (read the scripture). When Jesus said that He has overcome the world, it means that He can take your sad parts and make you whole again. He can help you be happy.

When Jesus said that He has overcome the world, it means that He will be there to help you with your sadness. Jesus gave us the church to help us. Jesus gave parents and friends and pastor and SS teachers… (as you share these answers, tape the heart back together.)

(Hold up the taped heart) The exciting thing about Jesus is that He not only tapes our heart together, but He gives us a new heart. (Bring out the second heart that was not torn). He can help us through our sadness and give us a new heart.

**Prayer:** *Thank you Jesus that you are there with us as we go through sadness. We thank you for all the people who you gave to us to help us get through our sadness. We also thank you that you mend our heart and then give us a new heart so that we can love you and love others. In the name of Christ, we pray, Amen.*

# Baa, Baa, Black Sheep

*"Baa, Baa, black sheep, Have you any wool:*
*Yes sir, yes sir, three bags full.*
*One for my master and one for my dame*
*And one for the little boy who lives down the lane."*

**Scripture:** "Share with God's people who are in need. Practice hospitality." (Romans 12:13)

**Materials Needed:** something made of wool, or some wool not made into a garment.

Any guesses what I have here? (Answers given—looking for the kind of material—wool). Yes, that is right, this is wool. Anyone know where wool comes from? Sheep, yes, that is correct. This is what we see on the body of the sheep. It is like their hair. What do you think would happen if the farmer didn't shave the sheep? The wool would grow so much that it would cause problems for the sheep and could make them sick. So the farmer shears or shaves the sheep to keep them healthy. Their fur or hair is what we call wool.

Now we use wool to make clothes. Wool is great for clothes because it makes very warm clothes. So, if you are cold, you want a wool sweater.

Now we have a nursery rhyme about this. (Share the rhyme). If you shaved a black sheep, what color wool would you have? Black of course. Now the nursery rhyme talks about three bags of wool. Do you remember what happened to the three bags? Let me share the rhyme with you again? Who got the wool? (Answer given). That's right.

Tell me, why would the person give away the wool? That's right, it is because they are sharing. Did you know that as God's people, God asks us to share as well? In the book of Romans, the Apostle Paul wrote in verse 12:13, "Share with God's people who are in need." We are asked to share with those who don't have enough.

What are some ways in which we can share? (At this point, highlight some of the programs at the church and in the community in which those in need are helped).We all can help. Even you, every penny and nickel, can help those who are in need.

**Prayer:** *Gracious God, thank you that you call us to be generous and to help those in need. May you help us to see who needs our help. We ask this in the name of our Savior, Jesus Christ, Amen.*

# Birds of a Feather

*"Birds of a feather flock together, and so will pigs and swine; Rats and mice will have their choice, and so will I have mine."*

**Scripture:** "A friend loves at all times, and a brother is born for adversity." (Proverbs 17:17)

**Materials Needed:** picture of a flock of geese.

I would like to show you a picture of some birds. Anyone know what kind of birds these are? *(Children's responses—look for the idea that they fly together.)* Geese fly together as they go south for the winter and north for the summer. Did you notice how they fly? Yes, that is right. They fly in a V They fly in a V formation to help each other. The bird in the front cuts the wind so that the birds behind don't have to work so hard to fly. They honk and honk *(honk like a geese)* to let the one in the front know that they support the lead bird. They also change which bird is in the lead so that no one bird is ever too tired.

Also, the geese fly in a V formation so that they can keep track of each other. It is to protect each other. Now our nursery rhyme talks about birds of a feather. *(Read the rhyme.)* What do you think the rhyme means when it says, "Birds of a feather flock together?" *(Children's responses.)* You are right when you say that they are like geese. Birds gather to help each other, cheer each other on, and also keep track of each other.

51

That is what good friends do. We make certain that our friends are okay and safe. We check on them so that they know we care about them. We also look to hang out with them so that we can enjoy life together.

There is a Bible verse about this. It comes from Proverbs. *(Read the scripture.)* The Bible verse tells us about being birds that fly together. We love our friends no matter what is going on. We take care of each other by helping each other when they are tired and worn out. We cheer each other on. Now we don't have to honk *(honk like a geese)* but we can cheer each other on. What are some words that we can say to help cheer someone? *(Children's responses.)* Those are great responses—we can help each other out.

**Prayer:** *Thank you God, for helping us with our problems. Thank you also for our friends who help us get through difficult times. We are grateful for those who cheer us on and for the chance to cheer each other on. We are blessed by Your love. In the name of Jesus Christ, Amen.*

# Birds of a Feather

*"Birds of a feather flock together, and so will pigs and swine; Rats and mice will have their choice, and so will I have mine."*

**Scripture:** "A perverse person spreads strife, and a slanderer separates close friends." (Proverbs 16:28)

**Materials Needed:** picture of a pig pen.

L ast week I showed you a picture of geese flying. This week I would like to share with you another picture from the nursery rhyme, Birds of a Feather. *(Show picture of pigs in a pigpen. Have some fun with the Children's reactions.)* Yes, it does look dirty. It may be fun if you like to get dirty. Now that I have shown you a picture of some pigs, listen in the nursery rhyme what it says about pigs. *(Share the nursery rhyme.)*

What do you think the rhyme is telling us? Hint! Hint! It is about friends again. Pigs like to wallow in the mud. Look at how dirty they are. What would happen if you came home all dirty and smelly? *(Children's responses.)* You could get into trouble if your friend caused you to get dirty. In the nursery rhyme, they are trying to tell you to choose good friends, not friends who will make life harder for you.

Does that sound like a good friend? In fact, the Bible says that bad friends can hurt you. Listen to this scripture from Proverbs. *(Read the Scripture.)* You see what God is trying to tell us is that a person who is mean is not a good friend. The word in the Scripture for that is perverse. The Bible also says that someone who lies will not be a good friend. That is what is meant when the writer said, "a slanderer separates close friends. A slanderer is a liar. This kind of behavior is like wallowing in the mud. It makes you dirty and makes it hard to love others.

Pigs also don't like to share. When you feed pigs, they all run to eat as much as they can before any other pigs. Feeding time for pigs is quite something, just make sure that you are not in their way when feeding time arrives. They don't like to share.

That doesn't sound like a good friend, does it? We want friends who will share with us because we like to share with our friends. So God is warning us to choose good friends, ones who will help us and not hurt us and friends who share with us.

**Prayer:** *Loving God, we ask that you help us to find good friends. May we also be a good friend, helping others. in Jesus' name we pray, Amen.*

# For Want of a Nail

*"For want of a nail, the shoe was lost; for want of the shoe, the horse was lost. For want of the horse, the rider was lost; for want of the rider, the battle was lost. For want of the battle, the kingdom was lost; and all for the want of a horseshoe nail."*

**Scripture:** "In those days John the Baptist came, preaching in the Desert of Judea and saying, 'Repent, for the kingdom of heaven is near.' This is he who was spoken of through the prophet Isaiah: 'A voice of one calling in the desert, `Prepare the way for the Lord, make straight paths for him.' "(Matthew 3:3)

**Materials Needed:** a nail.

Look what I have today. A Nail. What do you use a nail for? *(Children's responses.)* In our nursery rhyme today, it talks about the importance of a nail. *(Share the rhyme.)* Did you hear what the rhyme had to say? A nail was needed to shoe the horse. In those days, the horses wore horseshoes that were attached to the horse's hoof. It was to make certain that the horse did not hurt itself by stepping on stones. If the horse did not have a shoe, there was a chance that the horse would get hurt and thus the rider would not be able to ride the horse. In the nursery rhyme, the horse was the way in which people got from one place to another and how they fought in battles. The nail which was so small was necessary for a greater purpose.

The rhyme reminds us that God uses something small to tell others about His love. In the Bible, God used John the Baptist to tell others that Jesus was coming.

The Scripture goes like this. *(Share the Scripture.)* John the Baptist was dressed oddly. He wore burlap and ate locusts and honey. It doesn't sound like the most effective person to share the good news of the gospel of Jesus Christ.

This tells us that God uses all kinds of people to share the gospel. God uses ministers and Sunday School teachers and parents to share the gospel. God also uses you to tell about the love of God. Yes, even you! You can tell others about Jesus and His love. What are some of the ways in which you can share about God and Jesus and His love? *(Children's responses.)* Great responses. Yes, you can invite friends to Sunday School and church. You can be kind to all people. You can listen to your parents. There are many ways in which you can show the love of Jesus.

**Prayer:** *We love you, God. Thank you for sending Jesus and allowing us to be the ones who share that great news. Thank you for the opportunities that we will have to show others God's love and the times that we can tell about the love of God. We bring this prayer to you in the name of our Savior, Jesus Christ. Amen.*

# One to Ten

*"1, 2, 3, 4, 5! I caught a hare alive.*
*6, 7, 8, 9,10! I let her go again."*

**Scripture:** "And God blessed them: and God said unto them, Be fruitful, and multiply, and replenish the earth, and subdue it; and be stewards over the fish of the sea, and over the birds of the heavens, and over every living thing that moves upon the earth." (Genesis 1:28)

**Materials Needed:** recyclable items.

Did you know that you have a great responsibility? Let me share it with you. *(Read the scripture.)* Did you hear it? In the account of creation, we humans are called to take care of creation. We are to be fruitful in the sense that we have families. We are to subdue the earth which means that we are to take that which is dangerous and make it safe. What are some places that are dangerous on the earth? *(Children's responses.)*

That is right! We are to protect ourselves from hurricanes and windstorms. We protect ourselves from earthquakes by building our buildings stronger. Together we are to make certain that we work to keep our world clean and healthy.

There is a nursery rhyme about this. *(Share the rhyme.)* What are some things that you can do at your age to take care of God's creation? *(Children's responses.)* We recycle here at church, and you can recycle at home. What are some things that can be recycled? Here are some of the items that can be recycled. Soda cans, plastic bottles, and paper are some items which we can recycle. What color is the recycle container? It is blue. Here at church, we keep the recycle container in (*name the areas the containers are found.)*

Also, you can do something as simple as drink water from a reusable bottle. You can turn the water faucet off when you are not using it. Together we can make our world cleaner. This is one of the ways in which God calls us to take care of the world.

**Prayer:** *Dear God, we thank you for the beautiful world that You have given to us. We are blessed by Your generosity. From the gorgeous sunsets to the wonderful sky, we give You thanks for the many ways You touch us through our world. Help us to take care of the world that we have. We ask this prayer in the name of Jesus Christ, Amen.*

# Old Mother Hubbard

*"Old Mother Hubbard went to the cupboard,*
*To give her poor dog a bone; But when she got there*
*The cupboard was bare, and so the dog had none."*

**Scripture:** "But when you give a banquet, invite the poor, the crippled, the lame, the blind, and you will be blessed. Although they cannot repay you, you will be repaid at the resurrection of the righteous." (Luke 14:13-14)

**Materials Needed:** a bone or a picture of a bone.

I have a picture here. Any guesses as to what this may be? (*Children's responses.*) Yes, this is a bone. Now would you want this for dinner? Of course not. What would you want for dinner? (*Children's responses.*) That all sounds fantastic. I should have you cook for me.

Well, there is a nursery rhyme about an old woman who had nothing to eat. Any guesses as to who this may be? It is Old Mother Hubbard. Her rhyme goes like this. (*Share the nursery rhyme.*) The rhyme says that Old Mother Hubbard is so poor that she doesn't have any food in her house, not even a bone to give to her dog. That is very sad. And the sad thing is that there are people in our community who are like Old Mother Hubbard. They may not be old, but they do not have food in the house.

We have been blessed to have plenty of food. So how do we share food with someone like Old Mother

Hubbard? *(Children's responses.)* One of the ways that we help here at church is through our Food Bank. God calls us to help when someone is poor and hurting. *(Share Scripture.)* When you go shopping or you can look in your cupboards in order to find food to share. Then you can bring food to church, and we will take it to the Food Bank. What are some items of food that you think someone else would like? *(Children's responses.)* That sounds like a great food selection. The Food Bank box is located *(Share where yours is located.)* and the Food Bank itself is located at *(Address of your Food Bank.)* and is open *(Share hours.)* We are blessed to have such generous young people here at church and in our community.

**Prayer:** *Most Merciful Father, we thank You that You provide. You provide us with love and food. Help us to do the same to another person. As You have been generous with us, help us to be generous with others. In Jesus' name we pray, Amen.*

# The Cat and The Fiddle

*"Hey, diddle, diddle! The cat and the fiddle, the cow jumped over the moon. The little dog laughed to see such sport, and the dish ran away with the spoon."*

**Scripture:** "Be joyful in hope" (Romans 12:12)

**Materials Needed:** any of the items in the rhyme.

What are some things that make you laugh? What do you think is funny? *(Children's responses.)* Those are all funny things. In fact, it is great that we laugh. The Bible makes it clear that we are to enjoy life. We are to laugh.

Our nursery rhyme talks about this. Let me share it with you. *(Read the rhyme.)* Wouldn't that be quite a sight! A cat playing a fiddle which is a violin. The cow jumping over the moon. A dog laughing! And then while you are watching all of this, from off of the table, the dish on which you just ate lunch, the plate got up and ran away with the spoon. Wouldn't you laugh over that?! I sure would.

The Bible makes it clear that we are to enjoy life. We are to laugh. There are many Bible verses that say that we are to enjoy life, that we are to laugh. I would like to share one with you. *(Read the scripture.)* This is not the only place in which we hear about enjoying life. The Apostle Paul also wrote in the letter to the Philippians 4:4 that we are to "Rejoice in the Lord always. Again, I say rejoice."

When the Bible says that we are to rejoice, it also gives us a reason. The reason in which we can rejoice is that God is good, God is in charge, and God has saved us. We can celebrate because God will give to us what is best for us, even though sometimes it is hard. We can celebrate because God will take away what has been bothering us when it is the appropriate time. We can celebrate because God has saved us. When life is hard, we can know that God has something better awaiting us, heaven. The cross shows us that God has the best in mind for us as Jesus saved us from our sins and then rose from the grave to give us the power to love life. This is the hope that we hear about in Romans, that God has saved us for His glory and to His purposes.

For these reasons, we can rejoice. Like laughing at a dish and spoon running away from the table or a dog laughing at the cow jumping over the moon. Or we can laugh because God has saved us through the cross.

**Prayer:** *We thank you God for Your salvation. We are grateful for Your Son going to the cross for us to be saved. Let us now enjoy life in this hope that You truly do love us and that You care for us. In Christ's love, we pray, Amen.*

# Animals of the Bible

# God Rescues the Animals

**Scripture:** Genesis 6:17-21

**Materials Needed:** A shoe box.

What are your favorite animals? *(Children's responses.)* Each of these animals are incredible. Do you know who we can thank for protecting our animals and making certain that we can enjoy them today? That is right, Noah! God had asked Noah to build an ark to survive the flood that would be coming over all the earth. The flood would clean the earth of all the evil that had risen. But God didn't want all the earth destroyed. God would save the animals as well as Noah and his family.

Do any of you know what the ark would look like? *(Children's responses.)* We usually think of the ark as a rounded bottom boat. However, if we look at the description given in the Bible, we read that the ark was a large rectangular box. The description of the ark is found in Genesis 6. It is there that God describes the construction of the ark, and it would look like this. Does anyone know what this is? *(Children's responses.)* That is correct. This is a shoe box. The ark would have been shaped like this.

Scientists have tested the fact that this design would have survived greater than a rounded bottomed boat. In fact, it is nearly impossible to turn this over in the water. The Bible described the flood as a huge gushing of water from above and from below. The ark of this design would have survived almost any kind of water event. *(Show how it would have floated over the water.)*

Now through the ark, God saved a family, Noah's family, and all the animals of the earth. Let us think for a moment. Why did God save the animals? What do animals do for us? *(Children's responses.)* All your answers are incredible!

God know that we needed animals. We need animals for us to have food. We need animals for us to take care of them. We need animals so that we can enjoy them. We need animals because they are so special to look at and for us to see the incredible creativity of God. We see how God made so many different ones to show how great and magnificent and incredible God is.

**Prayer:** *We thank you God for saving the animals from the flood. We also thank You for being so kind to us that You gave these amazing animals to look at and to enjoy and for us to take care of them. You have blessed us greatly. In Jesus' name we pray, Amen.*

# Eagle

## God Gives Strength

**Scripture:** "And those who wait for the Lord shall renew their strength. They will mount up with wings like eagles. They will walk and not get tired. They will walk and not become weary." (Isaiah 40:31)

**Materials Needed:** Picture of an eagle.

Have you ever been tired? Really tired? Too tired to go on. And all you ever wanted to do was just sit and watch TV? What do you do when you are that tired? *(Children's responses.)*

God has said that when we are tired, really tired, tired emotionally, and there is nothing left, or tired spiritually, and you have trouble focusing, God's response is that we are to seek God. We are to look up to God and ask for strength, for help, and for guidance. The Scripture that shares that is Isaiah 40:31 *(Read Scripture.)*.

We will get strength like an eagle who is flying. *(Show picture of an eagle in flight.)* Here is a picture of an eagle flying. It looks great. They fly very high. It takes a lot of strength to get that far into the sky. This is the kind of strength that God is promising to those who seek Him when they are weary and tired.

Also, from that high in the sky, what do you think the eagle can see? *(Children's responses.)* An eagle can see far, far away by being that far above the trees and roofs and buildings. An eagle flies far above the things that make it hard to see so that he can find food. When we ask God for strength, He gives us the ability to see beyond our problems and see solutions and answers to our problems.

This comes when we go to God for strength. How can we go to God? *(Children's responses.)* We can take a nap to get our strength back. That is how God made us to need rest. We can find God giving us strength through the Bible. When we read the Bible, we are like the eagle, flying high above our problems so that we can find solutions. When we come to church and Sunday School, we are given strength through the fellowship here. When we pray, God gives us strength directly through our connecting with Him. So let us remember that when we are tired, to seek God, asking for His strength and guidance.

**Prayer:** *Almighty God, we pray that when we are in need, that You provide Your strength so that we can serve You. We ask this in the name of Jesus Christ, Amen.*

# Scorpion

## God Gives Good Gifts

**Scripture:** "And which of you if you asked for an egg, will your father give you a scorpion instead." (Luke 11:12)

**Materials Needed:** a picture of a scorpion

What is the last gift that you got either for your birthday or Christmas or a holiday? (*Children's responses.*) Those all sound like great gifts. Have you ever gotten a gift that was not good? (*Children's responses.*) How did you feel when you got the unusual present? (*Children's responses.*)

Jesus in the gospel of Luke told us about presents. In this passage, He was talking about presents that God gives us. To illustrate this, Jesus used the example of one of your parents, your father. Here is the Scripture that Jesus shared. (*Read the Scripture of Luke 11:1-9*) The presents that Jesus is talking about here is prayer.

Suppose that you wanted an egg from your father. You were really hungry for an egg. Your dad, listening to you, reaches out and hands you this (either a picture of a scorpion or a plastic one). That is kind of scary! I sure wouldn't want this to be on my plate for breakfast! Your father who loves you would never give you anything that would hurt you or harm you.

This story is about what you ask for from God. God is very generous and would not give you something that will hurt or harm you. When you ask in prayer, God, like a loving father, will share what you need for the moment. If you asked for an egg to eat for breakfast, God would not give you a scorpion. Instead, God looks to give you what you need.

One thing about prayer as well. Let us remember to ask for things that we need. If you ask for things that you don't need, God probably will not give it to you. God doesn't want us to be selfish and greedy in our prayers asking for thing beyond what is needed. God will hear our prayers and provide for us what we need to live in this world as His people.

**Prayer:** *Generous God, we thank You that You are so kind and generous to us. We thank You for the way in which You provide for our needs and how You watch over us. We are grateful for the way You hear us and how we are blessed by our relationship with You. We lift this prayer to You in the name of Jesus, Amen.*

# Snake or Cobra

### Mean People

**Scripture:** Psalm 58:3-4; The wicked go astray. They speak lies and are wayward. Their venom is like a snake, like that of a cobra that has stopped it ears to the tune of its charmer.

**Materials Needed:** A Rubber snake or a picture of a snake.

Would you agree that there are mean people in the world? *(Children's responses.)* What are some things that mean people do to hurt others and to hurt us? *(Children's responses.)* All these answers let us know that there are people who have not listened to God and have not followed Him. The result of ignoring God is that it is easier to do mean things, like what we talked about.

The animal in the Bible that shows us this is the snake. How many of you like snakes? *(Children's responses.)* What is it about snakes that we don't like? *(Children's responses.)* God has shared with us that those who don't follow God are like snakes who don't listen to their master. Here is the verse that describes this. *(Read the Bible verse.)*

The snake or cobra is an example of what happens when we don't listen to God. We are like an animal who ignores their master. We are to listen to God which helps us to be nice to people.

What are some of the ways in which we can be nice? What has God told us in the Bible of how we can help others? *(Children's responses.)* Those are all good answers. When we listen to God, we help others, and we are better for it as well.

**Prayer:** *Great God, we thank you that you ask us to listen and that you give us friends and family and the church and the Bible to tell us how to help others. We are grateful for Your kindness and Your love that we find in Jesus Christ. It is in His name that we pray, Amen.*

# Whale

## Life Wins

**Scripture:** Matthew 12:40 "Jonah was three days and three nights in the stomach of a big fish. The Son of Man will be three days in the grave also."

**Materials Needed:** a picture or stuffed animal of a whale.

Has anyone ever heard of a guy named Jonah? *(Children's responses. Let the children tell the story if possible.)* Jonah was swallowed by a great fish. He was in the fish for three days. Jonah repented. Literally he came to his senses, he realized that he had not followed God and then asked God to forgive him. The fish then vomited Jonah onto the beach.

The stories of the Old Testament tell us something about what happens in the New Testament. How long was Jonah in the great fish? Three days. Listen to how Jesus talked about numbers. *(Read Scripture.)* Jesus used the example of Jonah to describe how long He would be in the grave. Jonah was in the fish for three days. Jesus would be in the ground three days. Now in the Jewish way of counting, any part of a day would count as a full day. Jesus was crucified on Friday and placed in the tomb Friday afternoon. He was in the grave all day Saturday. Jesus was also in the grave for a part of Sunday morning. In the Jewish thought, that would be three days.

Jesu used the example of Jonah to show us something important. Not only is the number an important number but the fact that Jonah was in the belly of the great fish for three days was used to show that God can bring new life. Jesus was in the belly of the earth for three days. God raised Jesus from the dead after the beginning of the third day.

This is what we call the resurrection. The resurrection is the core of our faith. Jesus did rise from the grave. Death did not win. Life won. This shows that God is the most powerful being in the universe that He can raise someone from the dead. It also shows that if God is on our side, then we will have life in this life and in the next one as well.

**Prayer:** *Dear God, we give You praise that You shared the resurrection with us. We are grateful that we are blessed with life now in this life and guaranteed life forever. It is a blessing that we share in the life through Jesus and His resurrection. We thank you in the name of Jesus our Savior, Amen.*

# Natural Enemies

## The Kingdom Coming

**Scripture:** Isaiah 11:6; "And the wolf will dwell with the lamb, and the leopard will lie down with the young goat, and the calf and the young lion and the fattened steer will be together; and a little boy will lead them."

**Materials Needed:** picture of a wolf with a lamb or a lion with a calf or lamb.

Let me ask you a question: do some animals not like other animals? *(Children's responses.)* That is right. Some do not like other animals because of not wanting to share territory such as your bed at night. Other animals are natural enemies. They are natural enemies because some are meat eaters and other animals are plant eaters. Meat eaters are called carnivores, and plant eaters are called herbivores. What do you think may happen when a hungry meat eater finds a plant eater? *(Children's responses.)* It does not sound like a pretty sight.

Well, there is a Scripture that says there is a time coming in which these meat eaters and these plant eaters *(show pictures)* will not have problems with each other. The Scripture is Isaiah 11:6-7. Isaiah was a prophet who shared that when the Messiah comes to establish his final kingdom, then those who were enemies with each other, will now be at peace. Here is what is said by the prophet. *(Share Scripture).*

Jesus has come and died to save us from our sins. He rose from the grave to free us from our sins. He is now in heaven to give us the Holy Spirit to give us power to ignore sin and to be able to help others.

The reason these natural enemies will now be friends is that sin will be removed from this world. The Savior will set up the final kingdom and then completely remove the one thing that makes us hurt each other—sin. In its place, the Messiah will bring peace and calm. The animals will live as friends. We call this the Second Coming, where Jesus will come back and completely set up the final kingdom.

Doesn't this sound amazing? Now as we wait for Jesus to return, we need to work on being friends with others here on earth until the time that God sends the Messiah again. When someone is hurting, we need to be their friend. When someone is crying, we need to be there for them. When someone is hungry, we need to give them something to eat. You get the idea; we are the ones who will show what Jesus' final kingdom will look like now.

**Prayer:** *Dear God, thank you that we have our animal friends. As we wait for Your Son to return, please help us to do the good work that You bring to us—to be helpers and to be kind and to show others how to love. We ask this prayer in the name of the Savior, the King who we are waiting for, Jesus, Amen.*

# Bats and Rats

## God Will Protect You

**Scripture:** Isaiah 2:20; "On that day people will throw away to the rats and the bats. Their idols of silver and their idols of gold."

**Materials Needed:** A rubber mouse or bat. *(Hide the mouse near where you do the Children's Sermon.)*

Do you hear something? It sounds like a squeaking. It sounds like the squeaking of a mouse. Can anyone see a mouse nearby? Oh, there it is. How many of you think that a mouse is cute? *(Children's responses.)* They can be cute. What about a mouse with wings? Anyone know what that would be? *(Children's responses.)* That is right—we would call that a bat. Where do bats and mice live? *(Children's responses.)* You all are so on today—yes, they live in holes, and caves, and crevices.

There is a Bible verse about bats. It is what happens to those who are opposed to God and when they realize that God is real. It is Isaiah 2:19-22. Let me read it to you. *(Read the Scripture.)* Did you hear what the response of God's enemies will be when they see God? They will crawl in the holes where bats and mice live. They will crawl into those holes to try and escape from God. They will give up their idols and false gods because they realize that God is now real.

Let me ask you, "Is it possible to escape from God?" (*Children's responses.*) Of course, we can't escape from God. God is everywhere. I think that they are trying to run from God because they now see that God is real. Those who have not thought of God now find that they should have been thinking about God all the time.

Did you know that God thinks of you, all the time? God sure does. God has said that He loves us. In fact, the most memorized Scripture is about love. It is John 3:16, "For God so loved the world that He gave His one and only Son so that whoever believes in Him will not perish but have everlasting life." The enemies of God were afraid of God. They were trying to run away from God. We who have found God and love God, will not run away when He comes. In fact, we will run toward Him when He comes. We will want to see Him and hug Him and enjoy Him. We know this because God is love. He proved it to us in the cross. We know that God is love because of the resurrection.

**Prayer:** *We are grateful for the many ways in which we have known Your love. We thank You for the cross and the resurrection. We thank you for our family and our church. We thank you for our friends and our pets. You have blessed us greatly, Lord God. We share the message of Your love in our lives. It is in the name of Christ that we pray, Amen.*

# Dragon/Leviathan

God is the most powerful being.

**Scripture:** Isaiah 27:1; "On that day the LORD will punish Leviathan the fleeing serpent, with His fierce and great and mighty sword, even Leviathan the twisted serpent; and He will kill the dragon who lives in the sea."

**Materials Needed:** a stuffed dragon or something like a dragon.

We have lots of verses in the Bible that tell us about God and us humans. There are many verses that tell us how powerful God is. How powerful is God? What are some of the things that God can do? (*Children's responses.*)

Look what I have today! It is a dragon. What are some of the qualities of a dragon? (*Children's responses.*) Now do you think that a dragon is more powerful than God? A dragon is very strong. A dragon has flames. A dragon can fly. Who would win in a battle of God and the dragon? (*Children's responses.*)

We have a Bible verse that tells us about a battle of God and the dragon. In this verse, the dragon is described as a leviathan. A leviathan is described as a large sea monster who is very large and powerful. Who would win—God or the dragon/leviathan? (*Children's responses.*) The Bible verse is Isaiah 27:1. It tells us of the battle between God and the dragon/leviathan.

*(Read verse).* Did you hear? Who won? That's right! God won.

Now let us think for a moment. Why did God win? Why was God the victor over the dragon? *(Children's responses.)* The reason that God won is that God is more powerful. The name "God" means an all-powerful being. God means a creator. Since God has the power to create the dragon/leviathan so God has the power to defeat the dragon/leviathan. In the Bible verse, it said that God would defeat the creature with the great and mighty sword. The sword is the Holy Spirit. It is God's Holy Spirit that is the most powerful force in the world today.

**Prayer:** *Almighty God, we thank you that You are such an incredible Creator. We also thank You that You are the most powerful in the universe. Your power is not one used to hurt another. Your power is used to show love and used to defeat evil. We thank You that You love us. In the name of Jesus Christ, we pray, Amen.*

# Lion

Jesus is the King

**Scripture:** Revelation 5:5; "And one of the elders said to me, "Stop weeping; behold, the Lion that is from the tribe of Judah, the Root of David, has overcome so as to be able to open the scroll and its seven seals."

**Materials Needed:** picture or stuffed animal of a lion

There are many animals mentioned in the Bible. There is one who is mentioned as king. This animal is also the King of the Jungle. Anyone know who this may be? *(Children's responses.)* That is right. This animal is the lion.

The lion is mentioned as one of the animals which David as the shepherd guarded the sheep against. He used his sling to fight them off so that the lion would not get the sheep.

There is another place that the Bible mentions a lion. It is in Revelation 5:5. Let me share it with you. *(Read verse).* Now did you hear what or who is listed as being a lion? That is right. You heard that there will be a lion in the tribe of Judah. So that we are clear, Judah was one of the twelve sons of Jacob. Judah is one of the twelve tribes listed in the Old Testament. Judah is the good son who the Messiah or the Savior would be a descendant. The scripture that I read lists the lion of Judah as a title.

Now that I have given you the history, who is the Lion of Judah? (Children's responses) That is right! The Lion of Judah is Jesus Christ. This means that Jesus is the king. The Apostle Paul states that at the name of Jesus, every knee will bow, and every tongue will confess that Jesus is Lord. That Jesus is King. Can you think of what this means for us? What difference does it make that Jesus is King? (Children's responses)

As a result of Jesus being king, He can protect us and guard us. Also, because Jesus is king, He can lead us and guide us. He can show us how to live and when we should help another person.

**Prayer:** *Lord God, we are grateful that you have sent Jesus to be our Savior. We are also thankful that You made Jesus king. He is the Lord of our lives and can lead us and guide us. We thank you that He is strong and mighty and can protect us and guard us. We lift this prayer to You in the name of our Savior, Jesus Christ, Amen.*

# Lion

Peace Among the Animals

**Scripture:** Isaiah 65:25; "The wolf and the lamb will graze together, and the lion will eat straw like the ox; and dust will be the serpent's food. They will do no evil or harm on all My holy mountain," says the LORD."

**Materials Needed:** picture or stuffed animal of a lion

I have a picture of a lion here. What do lion's like to eat? *(Children's responses.)* That is right, a lion likes to eat meat. That would make the lion a carnivore. A meat eater. Now the Scripture verse for today, Isaiah 65:25, tells us that a time is coming in which the lion will no longer eat meat but straw. The lion will eat straw like an ox or a cow. Let me read the Scripture to you. (Read verse).

This is odd, isn't it? A lion eating straw just like a herbivore, a plant eater. The Bible is trying to tell us that there will come a time in which there will be no violence. God is telling us through the prophet Isaiah that the animals that preyed upon other animals will no longer attack and eat other animals. There will be peace in God's kingdom.

Do we have that now? No of course we don't have that at all. In fact, meat eaters still eat other animals. So, God is telling us about this so that we can see that there is another time coming in which all will be changed. In the Garden of Eden, animals did not eat each other. In fact, there was peace among the animals and with humans. This is one of the promises of God that there is a time coming in which all will be restored to what God intended—that we all would get along, animals and humans.

This time that is coming is the Second Coming of Jesus. When Jesus comes back, God will set up His kingdom on earth. With God fully here on earth, peace will be the result. There will be no more violence. We will all live together in peace, the animals with each other and the humans with the animals. Everything will be restored to what was intended in the Garden of Eden.

**Prayer:** *We are blessed, Lord God, to hear that You will restore the world to the way You wanted it to be. We will live in harmony. The animals will be at peace with one another. The humans will be at peace with each other. We praise You that this time is promised and is coming. We ask all of this in the name of our Savior, Jesus Christ, Amen.*

# Camel

A Useful Animal

**Scripture:** Matthew 2:1-12

**Materials Needed:** A plastic camel or a picture of a camel.

Do you know what one of the most useful animals in the Bible is? *(Children's responses.)* Those were all great responses but for today, we are going to focus on this animal *(Show the camel).* A camel. The Bible mentions the camel in many places. Do you remember any of those times in which a camel is mentioned in the Bible? *(Children's responses.)* Abraham had camels and traveled around on camels. His grandson Jacob gave camels to his brother Esau as a gift when he and Jacob met up again after many years of being separated. David had camels and used them when he went into battle and for long journeys. John the Baptist wore a camel skinned coat as his clothing.

The many purposes of a camel were that camels could travel effectively over the desert because they needed less water than other animals such as a horse. Also, a camel was very effective because it ate the plants that grew in the desert. The camel also could carry heavy burdens. They were strong animals which were easy to tame. The camel was a great animal for that area of the world.

The Scripture for today is about the wise men who came to see the baby Jesus. *(Read Scripture).* It is believed because they traveled over the desert that they came on camels. To see the baby Jesus, the wise men brought great gifts of gold, frankincense, and myrrh. Strange gifts for a baby. Yet these gifts were symbols of who Jesus would grow up to be. The gold meant that Jesus would be a king. The frankincense meant that Jesus would be a priest. The myrrh meant that Jesus would die a meaningful death, saving the world in His dying. It was the camel who brought these great gifts.

God created the animals for us to enjoy but also for a purpose. The camel was an incredibly useful animal which allowed the people of the desert area of the world to move safely and effectively even though it was hot and not a great amount of water. God knowing the great world that He created also gave us animals so that we can function in this world.

**Prayer:** *We thank You great God for the many animals that we have in this world. We praise You that You gave us animals so that we can enjoy this life and also so that they can help us. We send our praise to You through our Savior Jesus Christ. Amen.*

# Grasshopper

God is bigger than us.

**Scripture:** Isaiah 40:22; "It is God who sits above the circle of the earth, And its inhabitants are like grasshoppers".

**Materials Needed:** A picture of a grasshopper

Can anyone tell me what this creature is? *(Children's responses.)* What do you know about grasshoppers? That is right—the hop upon the grass. That is where they got their name—they hop upon the grass.

Now if a grasshopper looked up to us, what would the little grasshopper think? We look pretty big. We look large. In fact, we look very powerful. We look so powerful with our big feet and tall bodies—compared to a grasshopper.

Now when we look up to God, what do we think? How big is God? Remember that God made the universe and all that is in it. God made all of the animals and all of the humans. God even made the insects. There is a Scripture about this. I would like to share it with you. It is about grasshoppers and how big God is. *(Read Scripture.)*

When grasshoppers look up at us, we look huge and powerful. When we look up at God, God looks huge and powerful. The reason that God looks huge and powerful is because God is huge and powerful. As the Bible shared with us, God is larger than the heavens because God made the heavens.

Since God is bigger and more powerful than us, we can count on God taking care of us and helping us to solve our problems. When we lift our problems to God, God is so huge that He can help us.

**Prayer:** *We thank you great God for how you protect us and watch over us. We are grateful that you are bigger and more powerful than us and can take care of us. We lift Your name in praise, through Your son, Jesus Christ. Amen.*

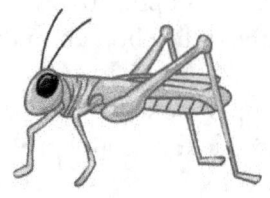

# Birds

## God Cares for us

**Scripture:** Matthew 6:26 "Look at the birds of the sky, that they do not sow, nor reap, nor gather crops into barns, and *yet* your heavenly Father feeds them. Are you not much more important than they?"

**Materials Needed:** a picture of a bird or a stuffed animal of a bird

We are sharing about animals of the Bible. One animal that Jesus talks about is a bird. Actually, Jesus said birds. Now what is your favorite kind of bird? *(Children's responses.)* This sounds great! Now did you know that Jesus used birds that fly in the air to show how we can trust our Heavenly Father.

Jesus told this in His Sermon on the Mount. He spoke these words to a large crowd in His most famous sermon. In this sermon, He told us about how we view the ten commandments, how we live in this world, and here how we are to trust our Heavenly Father. Here is what Jesus said about how birds show God's love for us. *(Read the Scripture).*

Jesus wanted us to know that God loves us more than birds. Now we see how God has provided for birds by giving seeds for the ground and fruit on the trees. The birds don't do any work to find food to eat. God simply provides food for them.

Jesus has told us that God will provide even more for us. God has also given food for us to enjoy and so that we are nourished through food. God has given us our family to enjoy and friends to have fun with. God has given us food to enjoy and games to play. God has given us a brain to think and a heart to feel love. There is so much that God has given us to show us that He loves us greatly.

So, when Jesus told us that God loves us, we can believe it because God has shared lots with us. Next time you see a bird, let it remind you that God cares for you.

**Prayer:** *Heavenly Father, help us to see that You can deeply for us. Every time we enjoy one of Your gifts, may we thank You in the name of Jesus Christ, our Savior, Amen.*

# Cranes, Storks, and Doves

## God Shows Us How to Live Through Birds

**Scripture:** Jeremiah 8:7; "Even the stork in the sky knows her seasons; and the turtledove, the swallow, and the crane keep to the time of their migration; but My people do not know the judgment of the LORD."

**Materials Needed:** a picture of a bird or a stuffed animal of a bird

When you go outside, how many birds do you see? They seem to be everywhere. The Bible has told us that these birds can show us how to live. Now I am not talking about the blue jays or black birds that you may see. The Bible says that cranes and storks and doves show us how to live for God.

Here is what the Bible has said about the fact that these birds know what God has taught them. Listen to what the Bible says. *(Read the Scripture.)* Here is what Jeremiah heard from God about us using the picture of the birds. He heard that the stork knows when to lay eggs and when to migrate. The dove, the swallow, and the crane know when to fly south and when to fly north. God is telling us that the birds recognize what God has placed within them.

Now this is to tell us something. God has placed within us the need and desire to be in relationship with God. We are to do the things that can draw us closer to God.

What are some of the things that we can do to get us closer to God? *(Children's Responses)*. Here is a summary of what you have said that can draw us closer to God: Read the Bible. Come to church and Sunday School. Help Others. Forgive those who hurt you. Follow God. Use kind words. Pray. These are all great responses. Thank you.

**Prayer:** *God You are so great, and we thank You that You want us to be in a relationship with You. We are blessed when we talk to You. We are blessed when we come to church and Sunday School. We thank You for our family and friends who help us. And we thank You for Jesus, our Savior. Amen.*

# Hawk

Listen to God and Follow

**Scripture:** Job 39:26; "Is it by your understanding that the hawk soars, Stretching his wings toward the south?"

**Materials Needed:** a picture of or a stuffed animal of a hawk

Today we will talk about a man named Job. Has anyone ever heard of him? What do you remember? *(Children's responses.)* Job was a man who experienced many sad things from family members dying to his business failing. So, what do you think that he should do about all this sadness? That is right, he prayed to God.

In talking with God, Job told God about his sadness and his pain. Job shared with God his fears and dreams. Then Job asked a great question. It is found in the Scripture. *(Read Scripture.)* How does the hawk fly? That is Job's question. How do you think the hawk flies? *(Children's responses.)*

Those are all great responses. Job's answer was that is how God made the hawks. He made them with the ability to fly. God in His wisdom made the hawk with the incredible talent of flying. This is how God made all the created order. Aardvarks eat ants, and beavers build dams, and deer run fast. Each animal shows the incredible amazing creative abilities of God.

We also show the incredible nature of God. We were made in His image and according to His likeness. As such, we show how to love as God loves. We show how to forgive as God forgives. We can show kindness and caring, just like God. As the animals show the wisdom of God, we show God as well in our actions and our thoughts and our kind words.

**Prayer:** *We thank You amazing God that in creation we can see Your incredible creativity. We also thank You that You made us to show Your love and caring. May we live like You here on earth. In Christ's name we pray, Amen.*

# Leopard/Cheetah

## God Helps Us Change

**Scripture:** II Corinthians 5:17; "Therefore if anyone is in Christ, this person is a new creation; the old things passed away; behold, new things have come."

**Materials Needed:** a picture of a leopard or a stuffed animal of a leopard or a cheetah AND a can of spot remover

What is the fastest animal on land? *(Children's responses.)* It is a cheetah. What does a cheetah look like? *(Children's responses.)* They have lots of spots. Lots and lots of spots. Now could a cheetah change its spots? Is there such a thing as a spot remover for cheetah? No, not really.

What if I used this can of spot remover? Could I take the cheetah's spots away? *(Children's responses.)* Well, I think that you all are right. I cannot take away a cheetah's spots. God made the cheetah in such a way that it has spots. It needs spots in order to hide in the grass and to be protected.

But there is an old phrase, you can't change one's spots. Now if we can talk about a cheetah or a leopard, could we change their spots. No, not really. They will always run fast and eat meat.

What about humans? Can we change who we are? There is a Bible verse that tells us that we can change.

It is II Corinthians 5:17. *(Read Scripture.)* The Apostle Paul was telling us that we can not only change but we need to change. We cannot stay as sinners. We need to change to become like God.

The way in which Paul mentioned this to us is to be in Christ. To be in Christ means that we take time to read about Jesus Christ. To be in Christ means that we are to worship Him. To be in Christ means that we are to have Jesus help us with our decisions and our thoughts and our lives.

When we are in Christ, we then can change—from a sinner to one who is saved. We can change from not knowing God to knowing God and being able to love God.

**Prayer:** *We come to praise You, Almighty God. Our hearts sometimes need to have Your love and we need to change. We thank You that in Jesus we can become new creations and can live Your life. We lift our hearts to You in Jesus name, Amen.*

# Animals of the Bible: Donkey

## God Speaks to us in a Variety of Ways

**Scripture:** Numbers 22:28 "Then the LORD opened the mouth of the donkey, and she said to Balaam, "What have I done to you, that you have struck me these three times?"

**Materials Needed:** a stuffed donkey or a megaphone.

L ook what I have today. It is a donkey. What do you know about a donkey? *(Children's responses. Highlight that a donkey is a beast of burden and that there is a cross on a donkey's back.)* A donkey is a beast of burden. The donkey was used to carry items for long distances as the donkey is a very strong animal. One of the times that we meet the donkey in the Bible is that the donkey is carrying Mary on his back as they road to Bethlehem. But today, we are looking at how God used a donkey to get our attention and speak to us.

Have you ever heard a donkey speak? That is right, they say Hee Hah. But there is a story in the Bible in which God allows the donkey to speak. A prophet named Balaam was asked to curse the nation of Israel. At first, he refused but when he was offered money, the prophet Balaam agreed to come and pronounce curses on the nation of Israel. As he was traveling to do this, an angel of the Lord stood in his way. Balaam who was still thinking about the money couldn't see the angel. But the donkey could. So, the donkey tried to go around the angel. When the angel moved to get in front of the donkey again, the donkey simply refused to move. Balaam beat the donkey but still the donkey refused to go forward because the angel was standing there with a flaming sword. At this point to show Balaam that he shouldn't go on, the donkey was given the ability to speak. Here is what the donkey said. *(Read the Scripture.)*

This shows that God speaks to us in a variety of ways. God blesses us with a beautiful sunrise and a gorgeous sunset. God gives us friends and family to help us with life. God gave us Sunday School teachers and youth leaders to tell about His Son. It is up to us to see the many times and ways in which God does show us the way.

Sadly, Balaam didn't listen to the donkey and went on anyway. Balaam is remembered as someone who heard God and didn't listen. We are blessed to have loving parents and a great church so that we can hear what God has to say and then listen and follow.

**Prayer:** *Loving God, we praise You for talking to us. We thank You for the many ways in which we hear Your voice. May we listen and then follow Your ways. We ask this in the name of Jesus Christ, Amen.*

# Deer

## Thirsting for God

**Scripture:** Psalm 42:1-2 "As the deer pants for the water, so my soul pants for You, God. My soul thirsts for God"

**Materials Needed:** a stuffed deer and a bottle of water.

God used an animal to describe how we are to love God. It is this animal. Anyone know what this animal is? *(a deer is the response.)* What do we know about this animal, the deer? *(Children's responses.)* They are fast. They can jump really high. The are marked or colored in such a way that they are hard to see in the forest. They do jump out in front of cars at times. And guess what, they get thirsty.

In the Bible, the book of Psalms describes the deer in such a way to show how we are to seek and love God. The verse reads like this. *(Read Scripture.)*

The Scripture begins "as the deer pants for water". The picture here is that the deer has been running and running. The deer is thirsty. His tongue is hanging out. He is panting so hard that he gets thirstier. What can help this deer? Water, like what I have there today. Water which can quench the deer's thirst.

Have you ever been thirsty? Really thirsty? So thirsty that all you can think about is getting a drink of water? And then when you get that drink, it feels so good.

This is how we are supposed to feel about God. We are thirsty for God. We are to think about God when we wake up and when we go to sleep. We are to think about God when we walk and when we stand still. We are to think about God in everything we do. This is what it means to thirst after God, like the deer pants for water. When we think of God this much, it will feel so good.

Some of the ways in which we can think about God is to pray at night and on the bus. We can come to Sunday School and have our teacher talk to us about God. We can do family devotions. We can talk about how God loves us to other people. When we do all these things, it will feel so good, like a drink of water when we are thirsty.

**Prayer:** *Almighty God, we thank You that You are worthy of our thoughts. We are grateful that You have touched us in our thinking so that we can worship You in all that we do. Thank You for being such a blessing. In the name of Jesus we pray, Amen.*

# Pig

Unclean Living

**Scripture:** II Peter 2:22 "It has happened to them according to the true proverb, ... and, "A pig, after washing, *returns* to wallowing in the mire."

**Materials Needed:** a picture of or a stuffed animal of a pig.

We have been talking about animals of the Bible. We now get on to an animal that is known for being dirty—a pig. What do you know about pigs? *(Children's responses.)* Pigs are known to be dirty animals. In fact, there is a Bible verse about this. (Read the Scripture—II Peter). A pig that is washed does return to the slop that it lives in. It goes back to being dirty. In this same section of the Bible, it talks about a dog returning to its own vomit.

In this Scripture, Peter is highlighting that sometimes people do not want to find God. They are told about God but instead of accepting the love and forgiveness of God, they want to go back to living as one who hurts others and hurt themselves. They refuse to live as God has intended for us as humans.

God gives us the chance to live better lives. Through the forgiveness of Jesus, we can be better people. With God on our side, we can be kind and generous. With God on our side, we can love others, even our brothers and sisters. With God on our side, we can love ourselves, and we can be better in terms of how we live.

When we make Jesus the center of our lives, we see people differently. We can see them as God sees them, as people who need love and guidance. When Jesus enters our heart, we can love with a heavenly love, the love of our Savior. And yes, we can even love those who have refused the love of God. They need to see a better way.

**Prayer:** *Almighty God, we thank You that You have loved us. We praise You that You have given us love deep in our hearts. We are grateful that Your love is so powerful and strong, that we can not only show a better way to live but we can lead others into Your love. It is in the love of Jesus that we pray, Amen.*

# Pig

God Protects Even our Eating.

**Scripture:** Deuteronomy 14:8 "And the pig, because it has a divided hoof but does not chew the cud, it is unclean for you. You shall not eat any of their flesh, nor touch their carcasses.'

**Materials Needed:** a picture of or a stuffed animal of a pig.

We have been talking about animals of the Bible. We now get onto an animal that is known for being dirty—a pig. What do you know about pigs? *(Children's responses.)* In the Bible, there are certain animals that were considered dangerous to eat in that day and time. One of those animals was the pig.

In the Old Testament, God has asked that certain animals not to be eaten. The rules were as such: any animal with a split hoof and does not chew the cud is unclean. That includes the pig and the horse. Any animal that eats dead things are not to be eaten such as the buzzard. Also, any animal that crawls along the ground is not supposed to be eaten. In addition to this, no animal's blood is not to be eaten.

The reason for this is that God wanted to protect the people of God until they were able to learn how to cook properly. The reason that we know this is that in the New Testament, the Apostle Peter is given a vision in the book of Acts in which God gives him permission to eat whatever he wants. It is a great vision in which a tablecloth is lowered from heaven and on it are all kinds of animals even the unclean ones that we just mentioned. God said, "Take and eat." Peter objects and is then told that all food is now clean. We can eat whatever we want except for blood.

This story tells us two things. One is that God does want to protect us. He makes certain that we stay away from things that can harm us until we are able to know how to cook properly.

The second thing that we learn from these about unclean animals is that as we grow spiritually, God does give us more freedom to make our own choices. God trusts us with greater and greater responsibilities.

**Prayer:** *God of freedom, we thank You for trusting us with our free will to make our own decisions. We are grateful for how You protect us and then entrust us with the freedom to follow more effectively. We give You praise for Your love, all in Jesus Christ, Amen.*

# Dog

## When is a Dog not a Dog?

**Scripture:** Psalm 22:16 "For dogs have surrounded me; A band of evildoers has encompassed me; They pierced my hands and my feet."

**Materials Needed:** a stuffed dog.

Do any of you have a dog as a pet? What are they like? *(Children's responses.)* Dogs are great pets! They love to lick you and go for walks. Dogs protect you and watch over you. Dogs bark and bark and often bark some more. Dogs love to let you know that they are there.

In our Scripture today, we have dogs as a symbol. Let me read it to you. (Read Scripture.) This is a story of someone who is in trouble. It is about someone who is going through a tough time. And it feels like for this person that he is surrounded, surrounded by dogs.

Have you ever been scared by a dog? They can be very scary if they are snarling and barking and showing their teeth. That is the story that we find here. The person is scared by the dogs that have surrounded him. There are other animals in this passage that are scary. In verse 21 the lion is opening his mouth and the oxen or bulls are trying to run at the person with their horns. This is a scary place. And yet, the person even though they see the scary situation, they are not worried because God is with them.

Let me share the next verse. The person then shared after saying that it was scary said this, "I will proclaim the name of the Lord. All who love the Lord, let us praise Him." Even though they were scared, they gave praise to God. How do you think that this is possible? Do they not see the scary animals? Yes, they see the animals, but they see someone who is bigger and greater. They see God who is bigger and greater. It is God who will protect the person even though it is very scary.

What do you do when you are scared? *(Children's responses.)* Those are all great responses. Next time that you get scared, try this. Try praying to God for peace and calm. Ask God to protect you. The amazing thing is that God will protect you and bring calm to your heart.

**Prayer:** *Great God, we thank You that You are able to take care of us and watch over us. When we are scared, may Your peace and calm enter our hearts and our minds. We ask all of this in the name of Jesus, Amen.*

# Fish

God can use the smallest thing.

**Scripture:** John 6:1-14 "One of His disciples, Andrew, Simon Peter's brother, said to Him, there is a boy here who has five barley loaves and two fish; but what are these for so many people?"

**Materials Needed:** a fishing pole.

How many like to go fishing? What do you like to catch? *(Children's responses.)* There was a little boy in the Bible who went fishing. He caught only two small fish that we know about. At least that is what he had in his lunch.

This is the beginning of the story where Jesus feeds a lot of people, over 5000 of them. Jesus had been teaching and it got late in the day. The disciples were worried that the people would not be able to make it home without eating so they wanted Jesus to send them away so that they could buy food along the way. To this, Jesus told them that they, the disciples, were to find food enough to feed the whole multitude. The disciples were shocked and frightened. How much do you think would you need to feed 5000 people? *(Children's responses.)* That is a lot of food.

Do you know how much the disciples found? A little boy's lunch with five small rolls and two fish. That is all they found. So, Jesus took the lunch, gave thanks to God, and then began to hand it out to the disciples. Do you know what happened next? From that lunch, Jesus was able to feed all the people. In fact, Jesus had food leftover. There were twelve baskets left over.

What this miracle shows us is that when we give something to God, no matter how small, God can use that which we give to a great purpose. When we share a kind word, God can use it to touch another person's heart. When we share, God can use our gift, no matter how small, to help other people. The fish showed us that God can use us to bring about His goodness and His love.

**Prayer:** *Almighty God, we thank You that You ask us to help You. You ask that we share kind words and what we have. Then You use our gift and us to bring Your love into this world. Thank You for using us. We ask all of this in the name of Jesus Christ, Amen.*

# Fish

The Symbol of a Christian

**Scripture:** Matthew 4:18-22 Jesus said, "Follow Me, and I will make you fishers of people."

**Materials Needed:** a piece of paper and a marker.

Do you know what the original disciples did for a living? *(Children's responses.)* That is right, they were fishermen. They fished for a living. While Jesus walked on this earth, they helped with His ministry and His preaching. They helped feed the five thousand and watched as Jesus healed people. But sadly, Jesus went to the cross for our sins. And then, God raised Him from the dead. After that, Jesus was taken to heaven to be back with God and to send the Holy Spirit in our lives.

When the apostles, these fishermen, began to share the message of salvation through Jesus, not everyone liked it. In fact, some of the leaders said that you can't share this good news of salvation through Jesus. In fact, they outlawed the sharing of the faith of Jesus Christ. They made it illegal to talk about Jesus. The end result is that Christians needed to share their faith but also needed to be careful.

So, they came up with a great way to find out if a person was a believer or not. Remember that the first followers were fishermen, so they used the picture of a fish to see if someone believed as they did, in the resurrected person of Jesus Christ. Today, I want to show you this symbol of what is means to be a Christian in the early centuries.

As they were talking with a person, the person who was a Christian would draw this in the ground or the sand. (Draw one of the loops of the fish symbol)
Then if the other person was a Christian, they would draw the other half.

(Draw the other half of the loop until it makes a fish.)

Do you see what this looks like? That is right, it is a fish. The fish was a symbol that we are now fishing for humans. We are sharing our story and the goodness of God so that others can see that we belong to a great and loving God.

**Prayer:** *Almighty God, You called people from all times and places to share Your great love. We thank You that You also called us to share how You have touched our lives. We ask this prayer in the name of our Savior, Jesus Christ, Amen.*

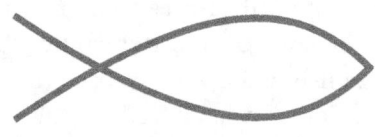

# Unicorn

Pride is serious

**Scripture:** Job 39:9 "Will the unicorn be willing to serve you? Will he bed by your manger?

**Materials Needed:** a beautiful Unicorn stuffed animal.

What is the prettiest animal that you can think of? *(Children's responses.)* What I was looking for was an animal that is big and strong, usually white, looks like a horse, has only one horn... (continue to describe a unicorn until someone guesses it.) That is right, a unicorn.

I have one right here. They are pretty special. They are strong and pretty. They are very rare. In fact, I don't know if I have ever seen one. Have you ever seen one? *(Children's responses.)* I don't think that they even exist.

Yet in the Bible, there is a strange word that we translate wild ox but means something like a unicorn. Let me read the Scripture to you. (Read Scripture). The word that we have a wild ox is in the Hebrew language, re'em. It means an animal with a single horn which means "unicorn".

There are nine separate verses with this word, re'em, in it. The one that we are looking at today talks about will this wild beast share a space with you and will this animal serve you. The verse shares that the animal is

111

too good to share space with you. Now if the animal won't serve you, what is his problem. The problem is pride. The animal is also too strong and pretty to serve you.

Pride is a tough emotion because it can get in the way of living life. When a person is proud, they think that they are better than you. Sometimes they think that they are better than God Himself. In fact, sometimes our pride keeps us from loving God and allowing God to save us.

There is one thing that we humans are not able to do ourselves—and that is to save ourselves from our sin. Only God can remove the stain of sin and the desire to sin from our hearts. The way in which God did this is to send His Son as a Savior. Through Jesus Christ and His death on the cross, God saved us from our sin. Jesus on the cross took the sin away and helps us to live without sin.

So, remember even though unicorns are pretty and strong, don't allow pride to think that you don't need anyone else. Please remember that we need God. We need God to live in this world.

**Prayer:** *Gracious God, we thank You that Your love is so powerful that we are freed from our sin. Your Son came so that we can live without sin and learn to love one another. In Christ's name we pray, Amen.*

www.ingramcontent.com/pod-product-compliance
Lightning Source LLC
Chambersburg PA
CBHW071019120626
46546CB00003B/1153